ÆTATIS. SVÆ. 20
1587

A History of
Fashion and
Costume

Elizabethan
England

Kathy Elgin

☑® Facts On File, Inc.

Elizabethan England

Copyright © 2005 Bailey Publishing Associates Ltd

Produced for Facts On File by
Bailey Publishing Associates Ltd
11a Woodlands
Hove BN3 6TJ

Project Manager: Roberta Bailey
Editor: Alex Woolf
Text Designer: Simon Borrough
Artwork: Dave Burroughs, Peter Dennis,
Tony Morris
Picture Research: Glass Onion Pictures
Consultant: Tara Maginnis, Ph.D., Associate Professor,
University of Alaska, Fairbanks, and creator of the
website, The Costumer's Manifesto
(http://costumes.org/)

Printed and bound in China

Facts On File, Inc.
132 West 31st Street
New York NY 10001

Facts On File books are available at special
discounts when purchased in bulk quantities for
businesses, associations, institutions, or sales
promotions. Please call our Special Sales
Department in New York at 212/967-8800 or
800/322-8755.

You can find Facts On File on the World Wide
Web at: http://www.factsonfile.com

Library of Congress Cataloging-in-Publication Data

Elgin, Kathy, 1948–
A history of fashion and costume.
Elizabethan England/Kathy Elgin.
    p. cm.
Includes bibliographical references and
    index.
    ISBN 0-8160-5946-2
    1. Clothing and dress—England—
History—16th century. 2. Great
Britain—History—Elizabeth,
1558–1603.
    GT734.E54 2005
    391/.00942/09031—dc 22
2004060882

The publishers would like to thank the
following for permission to use their
pictures:

Art Archive: 6, 7 (top), 8, 18, 22, 25,
30, 31 (top), 36, 39 (top), 41, 48, 53,
55, 57
Bridgeman Art Library: 7 (bottom), 9,
11, 12, 16 (left), 19, 20, 21, 23, 26 (top),
27, 32, 34, 35, 39 (bottom), 40, 43
(bottom), 44, 54, 58
Mary Evans Picture Library: 10, 17, 59
Topham: 14, 16 (right), 28 (bottom),
29, 31 (bottom), 37, 38, 43 (top), 46, 51
Victoria & Albert Museum: 26
(bottom), 28 (top)

Contents

Introduction

The reign of Elizabeth I was one of the most dazzling periods of English history. It was the age of Shakespeare, of Walter Raleigh, and Francis Drake. While at home great advances were being made in science, religion, medicine, poetry, and drama, across the seas explorers were mapping a whole new world.

Under Elizabeth, England enjoyed a long period of peace and prosperity. People had money to spend on luxuries, and more of them had time on their hands for leisure pursuits. It was the beginning of consumer culture, and clothing was the most obvious way of displaying the newfound wealth. Lavishness and ostentatious display were the watchwords, not only for the aristocracy at court but also for the rising middle classes, many of whom had made their recent fortunes trading the very textiles that were at the heart of the new fashion industry. In this mood of national confidence, merchants ventured farther abroad, trading English wool for silks, jewels, and precious stones in Venice, Turkey, Russia, and China.

Elizabethan costume became more lavish—more consciously elaborate—than in any period before or since. It was also almost certainly more uncomfortable, especially for women, who found themselves laced into impossibly tight bodices and imprisoned by huge ruffs around their necks. But men and women alike put up with it all for the sake of appearance. Walter Raleigh, though a shrewd and fearless explorer, was also a great dandy, only content when in the forefront of fashion.

Fortunately for us, the Elizabethan period was also the golden age of English portrait painting. Everyone who could afford it, from the queen down, dressed in their best clothes and had themselves painted for posterity, and it is thanks to these wonderful paintings that we know so much about the fashions of the day. We have clues, too, in the many church brasses and memorials erected to wealthy local benefactors in parishes throughout the country.

There were few, however, who cultivated their own image with more care and guile than Queen Elizabeth herself, and it was she who had the greatest and most lasting influence on fashion.

Chapter 1: Elizabethan Fashion

The Legacy of the Tudors

The fashion of the Tudors, in the years immediately preceding the Elizabethan period, was characterized by a horizontal, rather flattened line. King Henry VIII, Elizabeth's father, best shows off the fashion of his day in the many portraits painted of him. Henry looks out aggressively from these paintings, splendid but somewhat squat and top-heavy in a broad-shouldered, fur-lined gown with huge sleeves, flat velvet cap, and shoes with squared-off toes. The gown is worn open to reveal an ornate, pleated doublet and, of course, the codpiece, exaggeratedly large and ornate. It's an overwhelming impression of bulk: a solid and powerful masculinity offset by the softness of voluminous folds of rich, fur-lined fabric.

Members of Sir Thomas More's family are seen here wearing a mixture of Tudor and Elizabethan styles.

Tudor women's dress was modest, consisting of a one-piece bodice and skirt, or kirtle, worn under an ample gown which was open at the front to reveal the skirt. Necklines for both men and women might be either high collared or, more typically, low and square-cut, with the undershirt or chemise sometimes visible above. Almost every woman wore the angular "gable" headdress.

Renaissance Court

An astute, highly educated, and "modern" prince, Henry set out to create a true Renaissance court in London that would outshine those of France and Spain. This would be achieved not only through learning and culture but through the display of visual splendor. Henry encouraged the importing of fine fabrics—damasks, satins, and brocades—from Europe and obviously took great delight in wearing them himself.

From his wardrobe accounts, we know that Henry possessed "doublets of blue and red velvet, lined with cloth of gold," and one "of purple satin embroidered with gold and silver thread and set about with pearls." In 1535 he received a purple velvet doublet embroidered with gold as a gift from Thomas Cromwell. Some of Henry's clothes were said to be so oversewn with jewels that the original fabric could hardly be seen.

A Passion for Fashion

This period also saw the emergence of "fashion" as a concept. Once Renaissance thinking had placed man at the center of his own universe, individual personality came to the fore. What one wore came to be seen as a statement of this personality, or, as Shakespeare says in *Hamlet*, "the apparel oft proclaims the man."

This magnificent timber-framed Tudor farmhouse is just outside Stratford-upon-Avon, where Shakespeare was born.

More personal adornment, brighter colors, and fine fabrics were all ways of making this statement.

Under Henry's younger daughter Elizabeth, who came to the throne in 1558, the English passion for fashion would reach its highpoint. She loved fine clothes and jewelry as much as her father, but in her reign their display was to take a very different direction.

The headdress and hood worn by Jane Seymour, third wife of Henry VIII, echo the shape of the windows in the building above.

Dress and Architecture

Fashions in clothing often show fascinating similarities with the architecture of the period. The medieval period had been characterized by soaring spires and pointed Gothic arches, shapes which were mirrored in the excessively elongated and pointed sleeves, shoes, and high headdresses of court wear. In the clothing of the Tudor period which followed, the flattened shapes and straight, horizontal lines echo the style of their relatively low-rise and angular buildings. In particular, the gable headdress worn by a fashion-conscious Tudor noblewoman exactly resembled the flattened-arch design of the windows of her house.

Fashion and Politics

European fashion was generally dictated by the country currently in the political ascendancy. In the early years of the sixteenth century, France and Germany held sway and it was to their fashions for bright colors and extravagantly woven fabrics that Henry VIII had looked.

The Power of Spain

Already, though, Spanish influence had gained a foothold in England through two royal marriages— Henry's to Catherine of Aragon, followed by the brief and unsuccessful union of their daughter Mary Tudor with Philip of Spain. From the middle of the century, Spain emerged as the dominant power in Europe, and from 1556 onward it was to the court of Philip II that all eyes turned.

The rigidity of the Spanish court found expression in stiff, buttoned-up styles and dark colors, predominantly black, and these became the keynotes

The reserved, brooding personality of Philip II of Spain set the style for a dark and severe court dress.

of Elizabethan fashion. Curiously, even though political relations with Spain were tense for most of Elizabeth's reign, the English showed no less enthusiasm for the fashions of their enemy.

The Elizabethan Court

However, this was the golden age of drama, and enthusiasm for the theatrical permeated everyday life, subtly undercutting the seriousness of the true Spanish style. Queen Elizabeth encouraged the portrayal of herself as an invented character, never shown realistically but always as an allegorical figure. She was painted holding a rainbow or a symbolic flower: poets compared her to a goddess or to the moon—anything but a real human being. Living out

Queen Elizabeth's Wardrobe Accounts, 1600

Strict and detailed accounts were kept of the monarch's possessions and all expenditure in the royal household. From these we know that, excluding her coronation and ceremonial robes, Queen Elizabeth had at least: 99 robes; 102 French gowns; 67 round gowns (pleated all around); 100 loose gowns; 126 kirtles; 136 foreparts (embroidered under-petticoats); 125 petticoats; 96 cloaks; 91 cloaks and safeguards (over-skirts); 43 safeguards and jupes (jackets); 85 doublets; 18 lap mantles; 27 fans; and 9 pantofles (slippers).

this fiction herself, Elizabeth demanded that the men and women attending her should also be players in the on-going glamorous drama of court life. Artificiality was the watchword, and the more obviously artificial the better.

Fashion, for both sexes, went to extremes of design and lavishness, and changed almost by the week. Anyone appearing at court in an unflattering color or last month's fashion attracted her eagle eye and was a target for ridicule. Since being out of the queen's favor could be life-threatening, her young courtiers were kept in a constant state of rivalry for her approval, competing with each other in fashion as much as in the tilt yard or on the tennis court. All this attracted the disapproval of observers like William Harrison who, in his *Description Of England* (1577), noted that: "The phantastical folly of our nation (even from the courtier to the carter) is such that no form of apparel liketh [pleases] us longer than the first garment is in the wearing, if it continue so long, and be not laid aside to receive some other trinket newly devised by the fickle-headed tailors, who covet to have several tricks in cutting, thereby to draw fond customers to more expense of money ..."

Even when Queen Elizabeth and her court were visiting a great country house, everyone dressed in the height of fashion.

The clothing of upper-class women did not change radically in the first decades of the Elizabethan period, but there were two important developments: the separation of bodice and skirt into two distinct garments, and the gradual discarding of the gown. The skirt still fell in a smooth cone shape from the waist to the floor, while the bodice—sometimes strangely referred to as "a pair of bodies"—was becoming increasingly tight and constricting. Stiffened with stays made of whalebone, or sometimes cane,

The Spanish farthingale and false sleeves hanging from the shoulders create the typical shape of the mid-Elizabethan period.

wood, or metal, it fitted closely and ended in a deep point at the waist, which had to be as slim as possible. According to Catherine de Medici, regent of France and fashion dictator, a thirteen-inch (33-cm) waist was the maximum which could be allowed in polite society.

The Spanish Farthingale

To make the waist appear even smaller and disguise the hips, a new device called the farthingale, or *verdingale*, was developed. This was an underskirt into which were sewn circular hoops made of whalebone, wire, or wood. Increasing in size from waist to ground, they formed a bell-shaped cage which made the skirt stand out from the body. This style was known as the Spanish farthingale. By the 1570s it was immensely popular and was worn by women of all classes. A simpler alternative was the "bum roll," a roll of padding which tied around the waist.

As the use of padding made the female silhouette more unnatural, clothes became far more uncomfortable. Given that Elizabethan families tended to be large and women were therefore pregnant for much of their lives, the constricting effect of fitted bodice, narrow waist, and tight sleeves may have helped to account for the high rate of mother and child mortality.

The impulse to display oneself, however, overrode the discomfort. Between 1550 and 1580 the inventive

Lace Making

The most delicate lace was bobbin lace, developed in Flanders in the 1520s. This is produced by working together threads from several bobbins around pins in a stuffed cushion. The main feature of bobbin lace is the triangular edging resembling teeth, which gave it its French name, *dentelle* (from *dent* meaning "tooth"). Bobbin lace, although skillful, required no special tools and was therefore accessible to amateurs. Needle lace, invented by Venetian embroiderers around 1540, is produced by pulling threads from a base fabric to leave a mesh and then working buttonhole stitch across the spaces to form patterns. Because it required the production of a base fabric, needle lace was more of an industry, and the province of male professionals.

Elizabethans found seemingly endless variations on the basic garments of their wardrobe.

Necklines and Sleeves

Both high and low necklines were fashionable. A stand-up collar, open at the throat, topped the higher neckline, while in the décolleté style, the severity of the Tudor square neckline was softened into a slight curve. The chemise, which had earlier concealed the bosom, was increasingly discarded or replaced by a gauzy "fill-in."

Sleeves at this point generally emerged from puffed-out shoulders to fit closely along the arm, but there were many variations. Sometimes the puffing extended to the elbow and the rest of the sleeve was detachable; often the fabric was gathered into bands along the length of the arm. At the other extreme, the "bishop sleeve" fell full from the shoulder to a tight wristband. The curious fashion for "hanging," or false sleeves, which hung behind the real ones, gained popularity.

The huge and elaborate sleeves of this outfit conspire to make the waist look even smaller.

The outer skirt was usually parted to display an underskirt of different fabric.

Menswear 1550–1580

The Earl of Leicester, recognized as the arbiter of court fashion, is seen here in the latest style of the 1570s.

The basic elements of bodice, skirt, and gown, which made up the female wardrobe, found their counterparts in the doublet and hose of men's costume, worn over a simple shirt and perhaps with the addition of a jerkin. Throughout the century, Tudor men of all classes wore some variant of these basic garments. However during the Elizabethan era, there were many variations in the cut of the doublet and the length of hose, and there was also a radical change from the Tudor style of power dressing.

As Queen Elizabeth's reign wore on, the many young men with whom she surrounded herself became more dandified and self-conscious about their dress, which rivaled that of women. The new Elizabethan man's way of emphasizing his masculinity was to create an image in which formal elegance only lightly masked physical grace and athleticism. A small waist, broad chest, and—especially—a long leg were in fashion.

The Doublet

The doublet fitted more snugly and its skirt was shortened to give a long-bodied look. The nipped-in waistline dropped and, like the woman's skirt, was cut higher behind than in front, so that it dipped to a point. Doublets, magnificent on the outside, were stiffened inside by coarse fabrics like canvas and stuffed with padding down the front. This fashion reached its height with the peascod doublet, popular in the 1570s and 1580s, which swelled out to hang over the crotch. More padding went into the shoulders and hips, adding interest to the inherently flat male shape but making it stiff and inflexible, paradoxically at odds with the wearer's undoubted agility. The doublet usually had a standing collar, which by the 1570s was so high that it reached almost to the ears.

Sleeves and Legwear

Sleeves were the feature in which most variety could be achieved. Like women's, they might be close-fitting or wide and padded. They were frequently separate from the doublet, attached at the shoulder with ties. The shoulder seam was then padded into a "wing," which covered the join. False and hanging sleeves were as popular with men as with women.

Basic legwear was short pants and stockings. There were three options, of which the most common was trunk hose. These fitted close on the waist, puffed out over the hips, and were gathered into a cuff around the upper thigh. From about 1570, trunk hose could also be worn with *canions*, close-fitting breeches which covered the leg between the hose and knee. The third option of baggy, knee-length breeches was usually worn by the less modish merchant classes, until later in the reign.

All were worn with thigh-length stockings, attached to the hose by garters, ties, or "points." The padded codpiece, hallmark of Tudor virility, was already old-fashioned and dwindled in size until it disappeared altogether after the 1580s.

Not all the buttons outlining the front of this peascod doublet actually fastened: some were only for show.

Fastenings

Because clothing consisted of so many separate elements, ingenious ways were found of fastening skirts to bodices, sleeves to doublets, doublets to ruffs, and so on. Hooks and eyes might be hidden, but—making a virtue of necessity—many fastenings became fashion details in their own right. Long rows of tiny buttons fastened a sleeve or the front of a doublet, lacing crisscrossed the bodice, and elaborately knotted ties held sleeves in the armhole. Stockings were fastened to hose with "points," laces with metal ends.

Womenswear 1580–1600

It was perhaps the queen's own attempts to defy or conceal her increasing age that led to even greater contrivance in dress and makeup after 1580. Extreme, distorted body shapes were clothed in fabrics whose every surface was virtually obscured by complex embroidery and jewels.

By the end of the century, the French farthingale had created an increasingly fantastic female outline.

The French Farthingale

The female silhouette altered dramatically in the 1590s, when the Spanish farthingale was replaced by its even more extreme French cousin, much favored by the queen herself. The wire spokes of this wheel-shaped structure jutted out at right angles to the waist, and the skirt then fell sharply to the ground, creating a curious hobby horse effect. In order to soften the sharp line of the hoop, a frill of pleated or gathered over skirt was added, which only served to make the wearer look as if she were wearing a tablecloth. Skirts were often worn open to reveal a contrasting, and equally ornate, underskirt. Thomas Heywood, writing in 1590, was not the only one to spot the inconvenience of a garment that made women unable to get through doorways:

"Alas, poor verdingales must lie in the street,
To house them no door in the city made meete [suitable]
Syns at our narrow doors they on can not win,
Send them to Oxford, at Brodegates [Broad Gate] to get in."

The grotesquely wide hips were balanced by enormously padded "trunk" sleeves, cut wide from the shoulder and narrowing to the wrist in a leg-of-mutton shape. The already stiff and boned bodice was reinforced with a stomacher, a pointed, narrow panel of stiff fabric, embroidered or oversewn with jewels, which ended in a deep V shape, resting on the skirt far below the waistline. The waistline itself was cut lower in front, and this—when the angle of the farthingale was increased by padding at the back—gave the impression that the body was tilting forward. Skirts were slightly shorter, revealing shoes and feet for the first time in a hundred years. The whole effect was of women teetering precariously off balance.

New Attitudes

There is also a disconcerting sense that the clothes, already stiff and further encrusted with embroidery and jewels, could not only stand up alone but were by now, in fact, wearing their owners. Masks and fans were sometimes worn at court, further disguising identities and making women, in particular, appear even more unapproachable and formidable, like the queen herself.

Fashion on Stage

We know much about current fashion from a scene in Shakespeare's play, *The Taming of the Shrew* (c. 1594). Among other fine details we know that Kate's husband has ordered her "a loose-bodied gown with a small compassed cape, and trunk sleeves curiously cut [slashed]". This is obviously the height of fashion, but Petruchio mocks it:

"... 'Tis like a demi-cannon,
What, up and down; carv'd like an apple tart?
Here's snip and nip and cut and slish and slash,
Like to a censer in a barber's shop."

Many elements of male costume were shared by women, and the same areas of the body—shoulders, hips, and waist—were targeted for distortion. Especially toward the end of the century, it is often difficult to distinguish between a bodice and a doublet.

Since they were easily detachable, sleeves continued to go in and out of fashion more than any other item of clothing.

Menswear 1580–1600

Fashion reached a high point of artificiality by the 1590s. Clothing was full of details which served no purpose, a fashion typified by the mania for false sleeves, which hung down behind the real ones on doublets and gowns. More unusual details emerged in the actual sleeves, such as leaving part of the inner seam open in places so that the white undershirt showed through. As we will see in a later chapter, collars and ruffs became more and more fanciful.

Cloaks

The cloak was an essential addition to male dress, worn both indoors and outdoors and always on formal occasions, but rarely just for warmth. A serious courtier would be seen in a different cloak in the morning, afternoon, and evening. Mostly semicircular and flared from the shoulders, cloaks reached to the waist, hip, or calf according to the current trend, but were always thrown with studied casualness over one shoulder, and held in place by a cord under the arms.

Legwear

Toward the end of the century, trunk hose became very brief, sometimes barely visible under the doublet. When worn without *canions*, as in the

This elegant young man with curly hair and ultra-short hose is thought to be the Earl of Essex.

famous painting, *A Youth Leaning Against a Tree Among Roses* by Nicolas Hilliard, this revealed men's legs to an unprecedented (and startling) degree. At the other extreme, loose breeches, known as Venetians, were also fashionable. Cut with side seams, and without any padding, these had a more relaxed feel. In the next century, the trend would be to follow this development toward what we recognize today as trousers.

Modish Melancholy

Dress was often regarded as an indication of mood, and toward the end of the century there was a vogue for romantic melancholy. This was encouraged by the passion for amateur poetry and was much

Black and yellow were the colors adopted by fashionably melancholy courtiers around 1595.

mocked by the dramatists of the day. "Have you a stool on which to be melancholy?" asks a drooping courtier in Ben Jonson's *Every Man in His Humor*. The archetypal melancholy man wore black or yellow and adopted a languid pose, his doublet and shirt undone.

Costly Clothing

Keeping up with fashion was an expensive business. There are records of aspiring courtiers risking the loss of a whole family fortune through their debts to clothiers. Robert Dudley, Earl of Leicester, the queen's favorite and a famous arbiter of fashion, owed £543 (around $271,500 in today's money) for seven doublets and two cloaks, while the Earl of Essex owed a draper £736 ($368,000). They were outshone by the Earl of Arundel, however, who is on record as owing a grand total of £1,023 ($511,000) to forty-two different tradesmen, including mercers, silkmen, tailors, and embroiderers.

If Sir Walter Raleigh really did this, it was a truly gallant gesture—a fashionable cloak cost a fortune.

Trade Winds

To feed the hunger for novelty and luxury, Elizabethan traders ventured ever farther afield, bringing back fabrics and precious stones from all over the world. English geographer Richard Hakluyt, dedicating his *Voyages* to Walsingham in 1589, wrote of all the new places the English trading ships were to be seen. "Who," he asked, "had ever dealt with the Emperor of Persia as her Majesty hath done? Who ever found English consuls and agents at Tripoli in Syria, at Aleppo, at Babylon, at Balsara, and which is more, who ever heard of Englishmen at Goa before now?" He goes on to tell of ships which braved the River Plate, Chile, Peru and the coast of South America, Java, the Cape of Good Hope, St Helena ". . . and last of all return home laden with the commodities of China . . ."

Colors and Fabrics

Surface texture and appearance were very important in Elizabethan fashion. An interesting texture might be woven into the cloth itself, as in damask, a reversible fabric made from silk or linen with a pattern woven into it; or brocade, a rich woven fabric with a raised design, often worked in metal thread.

Woven damask like this was even used to cover furniture in aristocratic households.

Alternatively, a plain, dark fabric could be used as a background to be closely oversewn with precious stones or extravagant embroidery. The most popular fabrics for this were silk, and the satins and velvets which derived from it. When not embroidered or stiffened with padding, silks and satins had a soft, smooth finish which fell easily into flounces over the farthingale.

Courtiers might also wear cloth of gold or silver, woven with real metal thread; taffeta, a thin, crisp, lustrous plain-weave silk; and, for accessories like collars and ruffs, the finest transparent muslin gauze. Cambric and lawn were fine-weave linens used for the better-quality shirts and undergarments.

Fabric of Society

As with all fabrics, the upper classes demanded the finest weave, while ordinary folks managed with coarser cloth. Frieze was a coarse woolen cloth that was shaggy on one side. Fustian was a coarse cloth made of cotton and flax. Gaberdine was a kind of felted wool. All of these were used for overcoats and jerkins. Of the thinner fabrics, muslin was a fine-weave cotton, and Holland a similar texture of linen. Other more exotic names, now more or less lost, were Sarcenet, Tiffany, and Cypres—fine silk gauzes which "instead of apparell to cover and hide, shew women naked through them."

Fabrics often took the names of the places where they were made. Linsey-woolsey was a coarse woolen stuff first made at Linsey in Suffolk. Kendal Green was a kind of green woolen cloth made at Kendal in Westmore-land, although the best green was dyed in Lincoln and was consequently known as Lincoln Green.

Court Colors

The black, cream, and formal tones to which the bright colors of the Tudors had given way remained in fashion throughout the period, worn by both sexes. Sometimes they were enlivened with a touch of a single color, such as the queen's favorite, coral pink. Socially, however, color was a minefield of etiquette. Black and silver were the queen's particular colors, which she allowed only privileged favorites such as Sir Walter Raleigh to share.

The 1590s and the queen's twilight years brought an ethereal quality to fabrics. Very pale colors—pink, peach,

and silver—were the vogue for men, while women wore soft, shimmering, silvery fabrics covered with sequins.

Robert Sidney, Earl of Leicester, is wearing the pale colors to which the glory of the Elizabethan age finally faded.

Hue and Cry

There were curious rules about the colors people of different social classes were allowed to wear. Bright red and purple had always been reserved for royalty and the aristocracy, because the dyes were particularly expensive. The middle classes, longing to imitate, usually made do with a duller red or pink. So strict were these rules that they became a focus of social discontent. During the Peasants' Revolt in Germany, one of the demands of the working class was that they should be allowed to wear red.

Embroidery and Padding

The Elizabethan period was the golden age of embroidery. Household linen, wall hangings, curtains, and cushions were all decorated. As portraits reveal, however, the most imaginative schemes went into clothing. Often the whole bodice or skirt (or, indeed, doublet) was covered with elaborate stitching, incorporating pearls or other precious stones. By the last two decades of the century, surfaces were so encrusted that the actual fabric could hardly be seen. It is interesting, too, that this extravagance was continued outdoors in the famous knot gardens, where plants and low hedges created a kind of living embroidery.

Designs

In embroidered clothing, geometric designs were combined with images of leaves, fruit, and flowers, many of which carried symbolic significance or perhaps referred to the family's coat of arms. Braiding and metalwork flowers were appliquéd and stitched around with buttonhole stitch, while chain stitch was a favorite for the sinuous lines of the tendrils that linked the flowers.

Women's Work

Few ordinary people could afford the richly embroidered fabrics worn at court, which were worked by professionals. However, as embroidery was considered a suitably quiet and useful occupation for girls, all young middle–class women were expected to be accomplished needlewomen. Some invented their own designs. Other women, who wished to reproduce a particular pattern made famous on the dress of some court beauty, could purchase a copy of the design from a professional drawer, so the woman could embroider her own version at home.

Shakespeare's heroines Rosalind and Celia in *As You Like It* recall how they have spent their youth happily stitching together on a shared piece of embroidery, and there are many examples of highborn needlewomen. Mary Queen of Scots, Bess of Hardwick, and Catherine de Medici, wife of Henry II of France, all produced exquisitely worked pieces, a few of which have survived into the present day.

The extravagant silk-work on these fine gauze sleeves features stylized roses, carnations, and leaves.

The Bradford Table Carpet, with its stag-hunting and country scenes, is one of the finest examples of Elizabethan household embroidery.

Bombast

For all the richness of the surface, what went under or into the clothing was often, literally, trash. Padding, or bombast, came in many forms, all of it cheap. Cotton, flocks, wool, horsehair, and rags were stuffed into the bum roll, the front of the male doublet, down the hose, and into raised seams above the shoulder. As well as restricting movement, this was all fairly heavy—there might be over six pounds (2.7 kg) of padding in a doublet alone. Strangest of all the fillings was bran, which may well have resulted in serious social embarrassment if the fabric was torn and it trickled out.

The twin obsessions of padding and embroidery were curiously combined in a kind of three-dimensional needlework called stumpwork. Animals, people, fruit, and flowers embroidered in metal thread, were padded so that they projected from the surface. This technique, although short-lived, is very typical of the late Elizabethan and Jacobean periods.

Both this collar and the magnificent ruff opposite show how blackwork embroidery could be substituted for lace.

Blackwork: Poor Man's Lace

Blackwork featured geometric shapes worked in black thread on a white fabric. From a distance it resembles lace and was often used on collars and cuffs as a more economical alternative, sometimes edged with gold and silver thread. Catherine of Aragon, an enthusiastic needlewoman, is thought to have brought the technique from her native Spain and taught it to her ladies. In a famous work by the Spanish painter Zurbarán, *The Virgin and St Anne* (1655), the Virgin Mary can be seen engaged in blackwork embroidery.

Collars and Ruffs

Ruffs came in a bewildering variety, from the open standing collar (left) to the deep, closed figure-of-eight (right). The highly structured open ruff and wired head-rail in the center was favored by the queen.

The item which, above all others, sums up the artificiality and impracticality of Elizabethan fashion, is surely the ruff. Worn by both sexes, what began in the 1560s as a fairly neat single row of pleats two inches (5 cm) across had, by 1580, developed into a massive cartwheel, two or three rows deep and up to fifteen inches (38 cm) across.

Origins of the Ruff

This curious accessory had its origin in the drawstring neckline of the Tudor shirt or chemise, which was seen as a small frill emerging from the doublet. The neckband then rose into a small standing frilled collar, which then became a ruff attached to the shirt and finally detached itself altogether. Made of very fine, almost transparent linen, the ruff was gathered into pleats which were arranged in different patterns according to fashion. This varied from a single teardrop shape to a multi-layered figure of eight, and might have an edging of fine lace or

gold thread. The ruff was supported underneath by a wire frame known as an underpropper or *supportasse*.

Different Types

Men and married women wore full, round ruffs, while single women were permitted the variation of a fan-shaped ruff left open at the front, perhaps with a gauze *carcenet* (necklace) covering the bosom. Another alternative for them was the *rebato*, or high, wired collar, made of linen so fine that it was transparent, which framed the head. After 1580, men wore either the narrow stand-up "standing band" or—more popular at the very end of the period—the floppy "falling band," the latter usually worn with a ruff on top.

Mockery of Millstones

By the 1580s the cartwheel ruff had reached such ridiculous proportions that people could hardly eat. There are tales — though no proof — of

Starching

Ruffs were made from fine fabric which had to be stiffened by starching, or dipping into a solution of water and starch powder, made from wheat or corn flour. Starch was introduced to England around 1564 by a Dutch woman, Dinghen van den Plass, who moved to London to teach this new art. Her fees were very high: four to five pounds for each student wanting to learn the technique, and an additional pound for teaching them how to make the starch. (There were twenty shillings in a pound, and the average weekly wage for a laborer was about two shillings.) Country women learned to make their own starch from a plant called cuckoopint. In order to get the intricate folds of a ruff into the correct pattern, the wet, starched fabric was placed over heated sticks and left to dry.

special long spoons being used. Ruffs were commonly known as millstones and, like the farthingale, drew down disapproval and mockery on their wearers. For the writer Philip Stubbes they symbolized the frivolous vanity of the age: "They stand a full quarter yard (and more) from their necks, hanging over their shoulder points instead of a veil. . . . The devil, as he in the fulness of his malice, first invented these great ruffs," he thundered in his *Anatomie of Abuses* (1583), adding with some satisfaction that in a high wind, they flapped about like rags.

The care of such delicate items was crucial. Fresh water was needed for washing and starching, and open air was needed for the bleaching and drying. At the height of the craze, hundreds of washerwomen on the outskirts of London earned their livings by the care of ruffs alone.

There was little difference between men's and women's ruffs. The one worn here by Sir Walter Raleigh has a single layer but is highly ornate.

Hats and Caps

Women's hair emerged only gradually from its coverings. The Tudor gable headdress and the linen coif worn under it covered the hair entirely. The French hood, which succeeded this, revealed only an inch or two of hair. Varieties of hood were still worn into the 1580s, but were gradually pushed farther back on the head. Coifs, or linen under-caps, were worn indoors and for nightwear as well as underneath a hat, but as hairstyles became more elaborate the coif gradually disappeared.

Women's Hats

From the 1550s onward, younger women began to abandon their caps and hoods in favor of hats. On the whole these were smaller variants of men's hats, but the favorite was the taffeta pipkin, a jaunty item with a pleated crown and narrow brim which sat straight on the hair, decorated with jewels and feathers. As the chronicler Jacobus van Meteren noted in 1575: "Married women . . . wear a hat both in the street and in the house; those unmarried go without a hat, although ladies of distinction have lately learned to cover their faces with silken masks or vizards, and feathers."

The more practical middle-class and country women preferred a sort of derby hat, quite square and with a turned-up brim. Straw hats were worn by country women for outdoor work and traveling.

This neat and practical little hat could be secured to the hair with jeweled hatpins.

The copotain was universally popular and remained so well into the next century.

Feathers

Feathers became a passion. As sailors and traders returned from ever-longer voyages telling of encounters with exotic indigenous peoples, illustrated books were hastily produced, showing their costumes to a curious public. The feathered headdresses of the Native Americans held a particular fascination, and from the 1570s onward feathers were in high demand for trimming hats and making fans. They were also worn in the hair as taller hairstyles began to render hats unwearable. In *The Memorable Masque* (1613), George Chapman includes a chorus of Virginian priests wearing "robes tuck'd up before [in front], strange hoods of feathers and scallops about their necks, and on their heads turbans, stuck with several color'd feathers, spotted with wings of flies of extraordinary bigness, like those of their country."

Men's Hats

Upper-class men kept their hats on virtually all the time—indoors, on all formal occasions, while eating, and often while dancing. Brims and crowns gradually replaced the Tudor flat cap, although a soft, narrow-brimmed bonnet remained fashionable throughout the period. Professional men were recognizable by their flat-crowned, wide-brimmed hats made of felt, leather, or fur. The most popular of these was made from beaver fur and became known simply as a beaver.

By the 1580s, hats were getting higher, and the felt *copotain* with its high, conical crown was much in vogue. Court gallants wore it at a rakish angle or tipped it carelessly back on the head. It was extremely versatile: the brim could be turned up or down, rolled, or worn flat, according to individual whim.

Silk-lined and with elaborate bands, men's hats were as lavishly trimmed as women's, with jewels, badges, and feathers. Fastidious Brisk, a character in Ben Jonson's play *Every Man Out of His Humor* (1599), is saved from a sword slash by his hat band "being thick embroidered with gold twist and spangles." Fashionable hats were usually imported, but around 1570, refugee French and Dutch hatmakers moved to England and began local production.

This quite grand-looking gentleman wears a wide velvet hat to match his robes on what is probably a formal court occasion.

Boots and Shoes

For most of the period, shoes were made in slip-on styles, with rounded toes and flat heels. Women's shoes were generally simpler than men's because, until the French farthingale lifted hems a little at the end of the century, they were generally hidden by long skirts.

These high-heeled women's shoes are from the end of the sixteenth century.

These slashed men's shoes would reveal highly colored stockings worn underneath.

Upper-Class Footwear

The nobility, who spent most of their time indoors, tended to wear delicate and impractical footwear. Slippers and pumps were made of leather, cloth, or velvet, and had cork soles. They were decorated with pom-poms or rosettes attached to the fronts, or by slashing the leather to reveal the colored stockings worn underneath.

Philip Stubbes, in his *Anatomy of Abuses,* could not resist pointing out the impracticalities: "They have corked shooes and fine pantofles, which beare them up a finger or two from the ground . . . raced, carved, cut, and stitched all over with silk and laid on with gold, silver and such like . . . to go abroad in them is rather a let or hindrance to a man than otherwise . . ."

When ladies and gentlemen had to venture out, they wore overshoes. Wooden pattens or clogs, known as chopines, could be slipped on over ordinary shoes in bad weather, or to negotiate streets which were frequently filled with filthy water. The shoe fitted into the toe piece of the chopine, and the raised wooden sole—sometimes several inches in height—kept the shoe clear of mud. They were, however, difficult to walk in.

Boots

Boots were originally worn only for riding or by the military. However, by about 1580, boots had become fashionable for civilian day wear, although they were rarely worn indoors. Some were highly decorative, with laced fastenings at the side. The best—made from softened and tooled leather—came from Cordoba in Spain and were

Slashing

Slashing was the technique of making cuts in one fabric so that lining of a contrasting color could be seen underneath. While slashed shoes revealed stockings, on clothing the under-fabric was frequently pulled through the slits for better effect. Slashing is thought to have originated in military wear, when soldiers made cuts in their leather tunics for better flexibility. Slashing was at its height in the early years of the sixteenth century, but remained fashionable throughout the Elizabethan period.

very close fitting to reveal shapely calves. Falstaff, in Shakespeare's *Henry IV,* refers to someone who "wears his boots very smooth, like unto the sign of his leg."

Others were enormously wide, reaching to the thigh with turnover tops, and were either slashed or folded into decorative pleats or wrinkles. These wide boots were usually worn with breeches rather than with close-fitting hose, and must have been extremely impractical for any real outdoor activity.

Country Styles

In the country, most people wore startups, a cross between a high-fitting shoe and leggings, which gave some protection from mud and weather. For more serious outdoor pursuits like fishing and hunting, men wore long leather leggings or high boots known as cockers.

Late Elizabethan Fashions

Built-up, wedge-shaped heels, made of layers of cork, were coming into fashion by the 1590s. Separate heels developed later, but during the reign of James I they were to reach the

dizzy height of two or three inches (5–7.5 cm) and were much mocked. By 1580, slip-ons had given way to tie-up shoes, with straps or ribbon tying over the tongue.

The skilled workers in this cobbler's workshop demonstrate the various stages of cutting, shaping, and stitching shoes.

Accessories

The quest for novelty produced a variety of ever-changing accessories, few of which were ever put to the practical use for which they were intended.

Gloves

Most fashionable people had at least two pairs of gloves.

The everyday pair were of plain leather in a neutral color with short cuffs turned back to show a lining. However, etiquette demanded another, much more elaborate pair to be reserved for display. Lined with silk and with their elongated gauntlets heavily embroidered and edged with lace or fringe, these were carried in the hand or tucked into a belt. The ultra-fashionable courtier wore one and carried the other. Particularly desirable were perfumed gloves, made from the finest leather and imported from Spain—although the thrifty might perfume their own with essences bought from an apothecary.

Handkerchiefs

The handkerchief was still a luxury and rarely came near the nose. Made of fine linen, embroidered, and lace-

Mittens like these—far too good for wearing—would be held to indicate status in a formal portrait.

Queen Elizabeth's feathered fan was used to hide the face from public view as well as to waft cool air.

edged, it was carried in the hand or carefully tucked into a sleeve or a pocket. Embroidered with flowers or initials, they were often exchanged as tokens of love or esteem. Shakespeare reflects this in the tragedy of *Othello*, which unfolds when the jealous Othello suspects his wife of parting with the handkerchief which had been one of his first gifts to her.

Belts and Girdles

One of the few items that did serve a practical purpose was the belt or girdle worn by both sexes. As well as emphasizing the fashionably small waist, it could also carry several small personal items such as a purse, keys, a small book, a perfume bottle, a tiny looking glass, or a fan, each hanging by a gold chain or cords. Men carried their daggers there. Scarves or sashes could also be worn around the waist or sometimes across the chest.

Purses and Pouches

Because few clothes had pockets, purses or pouches were essential items. Round or square, made of leather or silk, they dangled low on the hip and were highly decorative,

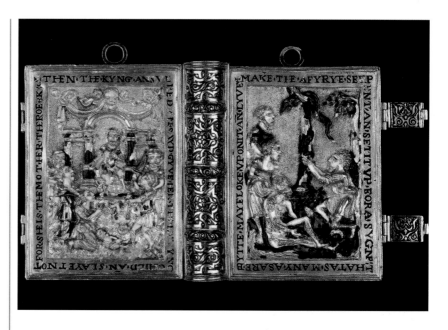

often finished with hanging tassels. Plain leather pouches were considered the property of old men.

Also hanging from a woman's girdle would be a pomander, a gold filigree sphere filled with perfume or sweet herbs which was carried to ward off plague. The word comes from the French *pomme* (apple) and a scent called *pomme d'ambre*. The equivalent accessory for a man was a pouncet-box, a small container with a perforated lid which held snuff or medicinal herbs.

The hooks at the top of this exquisitely jeweled prayer book show that it would have been hung from a woman's girdle.

Garters

Perhaps the most important male accessory was the garter, a small sash tied just below the knee to hold up the stocking. Men's legs were regarded as their best attribute, and garters were highly elaborate and often trimmed with jewels. Women's garters, being unseen, were less decorative. In *Twelfth Night*, Shakespeare makes fun of a passing craze for elaborate "cross-gartering" when he has the usually staid Malvolio adopt it in an attempt to please his employer. However, stage directors who wind the legs with ribbons in a crisscross pattern get it wrong. Cross-gartering meant tying a ribbon under the knee, winding it around the back of the leg and tying it in a large bow above the knee. This was quite a difficult style to walk in.

Chapter 3: Fashion and Society

The Royal Exchange

In 1571, trading in London was revolutionized with the opening of Sir Thomas Gresham's new Royal Exchange, the very first "shopping mall" in England. The Exchange, an elegant classical building modeled on the Bourse at Antwerp, was primarily a center of commerce, where merchants and tradesmen could do business. The cloth trade was prominent—the site had been provided partly by the Worshipful Company of Mercers, a trade association for exporters of wool and importers of velvet, silk, and other luxurious fabrics—but other trades were represented. Most importantly, the venture was to be financed by roughly a hundred shops offered for rent on the upper floors.

Sir Thomas Gresham, founder of the Royal Exchange, depicted in respectable old age.

The Exchange was functioning by 1567, but in 1571 it was officially opened by Queen Elizabeth, who gave it the royal title. The queen's visit had a galvanizing effect: tradespeople clamored to open shops, and the Exchange swiftly became the place to buy fabric, ready-made clothing, accessories, and all kinds of luxury goods. It was also the fashionable place to be seen, to stroll, meet friends, and show off one's new outfit.

Sir Thomas Gresham

The son of a wealthy merchant family in the cloth trade (his father had supplied Henry VIII with velvet), Thomas Gresham (1519–1579) was financial adviser to Edward VI, Queen Mary, and then Queen Elizabeth. Before the establishment of a proper banking system, the crown depended on loans and credit from rich merchants. Gresham's judicious advice on trade, the stock market, and currency reform restored England's tottering finances and earned him a knighthood in 1559 and a substantial personal fortune. As he had no heirs, he subsequently used this to found the Royal Exchange and Gresham College, the first college of further education in London, where free lectures on divinity, music, law, and the sciences were offered.

The Rise of the Fashion Industry

Different districts of London had always specialized in particular commodities. John Stowe's *Survey of London* (1603) tells us that: Cheapside was the stylish place for luxury fabrics and jewelry; mercers and haberdashers could be found in West Cheape and London Bridge; goldsmiths in Gutherons Lane; drapers around Lombard Street and Cornhill; and wigmakers in Silver Street. Those in

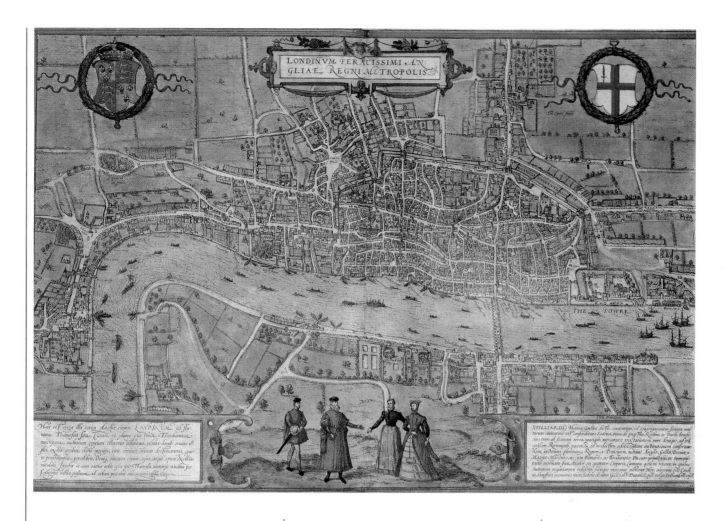

LONDINVM·FERACISSIMI·ANGLIAE·REGNI·METROPOLIS

search of food found their grocers in Bucklesberrie, fishmongers in Thames Street, and brewers down by the river.

The Exchange offered one-stop-shopping. Here were milliners, feather shops, wigmakers, imported accessories, embroidered goods, perfumes, and starches. And the tradespeople who offered sewing, starching, dyeing, and other services could all be found here. Ladies could also buy embroidery patterns, or have a drawer copy one for them.

Secondhand Clothing

Used clothing could also be bought in Birchin Lane. This was a serious

industry, especially among the poor for whom clothing was part of the everyday economy. Buying clothes secondhand, however, could be a risky business. In times of plague, the fleas which carried the deadly virus lived on in the garments and were transferred to their new owners. Since the poor who were buying the secondhand clothing lived in desperately overcrowded conditions, the plague spread like wildfire. The authorities tried to police the secondhand business, but traders were unscrupulous: one Marian Burrough was arrested because "she doth run into infected houses and buyeth clothes from them."

A plan of London around 1580 also shows people in the costume of the period.

Queen Elizabeth being received by Thomas Gresham at the grand opening of the Exchange in 1571.

The New Middle Classes

The majority of English people still lived in the countryside or in small towns and had neither access to the delights available at court nor, on the whole, money to enjoy them. However, the newly affluent middle classes were an increasing power in the land and they were keen to show off their wealth.

Sensible Clothes

They remained a few years behind the current fashions, and the fabrics they wore were less exotic and more suited to the practicalities of going about one's business in variable weather. Imported silks and satins were for the wealthy few: the urban middle classes tended to favor English wool and linen in subdued colors like gray and brown. A country gentleman was more likely to wear breeches than short hose, and his wife, a bodice and skirt cut plainly.

Comparing the middle-class attitude to dress to the madness of court fashion, William Harrison found them reassuringly grounded in common sense: "Of all estates our merchants do least alter their attire, and therefore are most to be commended; for albeit that which they wear be very fine and costly, yet in form and color it representeth a great piece of the ancient gravity appertaining to citizens and burgesses . . ." Their wives, however, "both in attire and costly housekeeping, cannot tell when and how to make an end . . ." In the growing middle-class towns, dress was still a major way of displaying social distinction.

Aristocrats out for a day's enjoyment mingle with the middle classes and ordinary London folk south of the river in Bermondsey.

Dedicated Followers of Fashion

Merchants who went to London on business were instructed by wives and daughters to write home about the fashions they saw, and were given shopping lists of suitable fabrics and accessories to bring home. One Philip Gawdy, visiting the capital in 1587 with such instructions from his sister Anne, could only write home in manly bewilderment at the variety on offer. Women had their clothes made from pattern books by the tailor in their home town and finished at home with trimmings from the local haberdasher. Unfortunate fashion mistakes were an easy and frequent target for satirical playwrights commenting on the social climbing of smalltown people.

Clothing was sometimes used as a form of money. The woman of the house might pay peddlers or itinerant laborers in cast–off clothing or food rather than in cash, while clothing and household linen were pawned or sold at times of need.

Middle-class folk generally wore clothes a little behind the fashion of court gallants.

Thrift and Recycling

Thrift was a middle-class necessity. Good cloth garments could last several generations if properly cared for, and household manuals were full of tips on cleaning and keeping textiles safe from moths. Adult garments were regularly cut down to make children's clothes, and household linens were refashioned into clothing. In a legal dispute over a family inheritance, we read that one Elizabeth Busby had acquired: "one facecloth whereof she made an apron, one tablecloth [with] which she made smocks, and two ruffs, part whereof she cut for herself, and part whereof she sold to the said Hitchman's wife, as also a hood which she converted to a coif, and another piece of linen which she made a neckcloth of. . . ." Recycling was common even among royalty. When her sister Mary died, Queen Elizabeth I had Mary's expensive clothing remade into dresses for herself. Elizabeth's own clothing was regularly remodeled and resized as fashion and her size changed.

Country Folk

The gardeners in this traditional walled garden are wearing the clothes of the general manual worker.

Working-class clothing hardly changed at all during the sixteenth century and, in fact, had altered little since medieval times. Women wore a simple skirt and bodice, with an apron on top and a kerchief over the shoulders. Men dressed in knee-length breeches and a shirt, or a simple tunic known as a cote, with a sleeveless leather over-jerkin. Both wore the leather shoes known as startups. Straw hats and bonnets replaced hats, usually with wide brims to provide shade from the sun. There was little choice of fabric, with coarse wool, flannel, or russet serving most purposes.

Men usually worked in their shirts and plain hose. Stockings might be cut from cloth in the old way, or knitted from coarse wool, but they were always worn: being bare-legged was a sign of the direst poverty.

Homemade Clothing

With no access to shops, people were obliged to make their own clothing from cloth, either spun and woven locally or bought cheaply at the local fair or from a traveling peddler. It was the woman's job to produce clothing for the family as well as its food, and women of all ages were skilled in spinning and sewing. They used their spare time for useful labor, some selling their surplus textiles for cash. Poor women also prepared flax and hemp for making into linen and canvas.

Despite their lack of means, rural folk had aspirations too, however limited. The word tawdry, meaning cheap and tacky, comes from Tawdry lace, the cheap, showy ribbons worn by country girls to trim their plain clothing. The name derived from Saint Audrey's, one of the regular fairs where such trinkets were for sale.

Straw Hats

The technique of making straw hats came to England from northern Italy in the sixteenth century. The word milliner, for a maker of women's hats, was first recorded in 1529, referring to the products for which the town of Milan was well known: ribbons, gloves, and elegant straw hats. Haberdashers who imported the hats were called Millaners, from which the word was eventually derived. By the mid-sixteenth century the making of more everyday hats from plaited straw was established in the southern counties of England, where the best wheat straw grew. A traveler noted that in Hertfordshire in 1735 he was told "that £200 a week has been turn'd [earned] in a market day in straw hats only, which manufacture has thriv'd in those parts above a hundred years."

Aristocrats and countrymen worked together on hunting expeditions.

Best Clothes

Although she probably never had a wedding ring, a girl would make herself a new gown to be married in, and most men had a "best" working shirt to wear at festivals. These were of natural or bleached linen and decorated with smocking, a kind of embroidery known in country areas since medieval times. Fabric was gathered or pleated to give extra thickness over the shoulders, chest, and cuffs, and embroidery was worked over the gathers. Designs differed from one region of the country to another, and many were remarkably complex.

When country people did venture up to town, they were immediately recognizable by their clothing and were an easy target for confidence tricksters. Such encounters feature regularly in the plays of satirical playwrights like Ben Jonson. One of his characters, young Squire Cokes from Harrow (then a rural area), is easily separated from his purse by the tricksters who throng to Bartholomew Fair.

Anyone engaged in outdoor manual work needed the protection of leather and stout woolen cloth.

Children's Clothes

The four elder children of Lord Cobham, seen here at dinner, are wearing obvious male and female clothing but the two toddlers on the left could be either boys or girls.

Babies

Children spent their first year clad in a shirt and diaper, or tailclout, and tightly wrapped up in swaddling clothes. These were quite restricting and were removed at various times during the day to give the limbs some freedom. They also wore a biggin, which was a small cap similar to the coif. If carried outdoors, they might wear a mantle. Babies are often shown clutching a stick or a ring of coral, which served as a teething aid but was also a symbol of good luck. Perhaps they needed it. One in five babies did not survive their first year, and of the rest a quarter did not reach their tenth birthday.

Small Children

Once out of swaddling clothes, boys up to the age of six were dressed in an ankle-length gown which had hanging sleeves, or streamers, by which they could be held while learning to walk. Girls wore a similar long gown consisting of a bodice and skirt. The clothes of even small children like these were frequently of surprisingly heavy and ornate materials. A little girl might wear an apron over the skirt of her gown for

Playthings

The toys and playthings available to Elizabethan children were rarely frivolous. Play was training for adult life, and gender stereotyping was obvious. Girls were given dolls to dress in preparation for the motherhood which lay not too far ahead, and even quite small boys carried miniature rapiers and daggers. King Leontes in Shakespeare's *The Winter's Tale* gives a charming description of himself as a little boy: "unbreech'd,/In my green velvet coat; my dagger muzzled/Lest it should bite its master . . ." Boys learned to ride early and enjoyed hunting, while girls learned embroidery as soon as they could manage a needle.

protection, but this was often embroidered, as was the toddler's bib and the handkerchief, or muckminder, which was pinned to the gown or tucked into the girdle.

Dressing like Adults

As soon as possible, children were dressed in miniature versions of adult clothes and were expected to behave accordingly. In many family portraits, very small children are shown as exact replicas of their parents. Some were allowed the luxury of wearing soft turnover collars for a few years, but a painting by Isaac Oliver shows a little girl of just four looking reasonably content in a proper miniature ruff. Given that their clothes were also starched and padded just like the adult versions, any kind of robust playtime must have been very difficult.

Accessories

Children always wore caps or coifs indoors. Once outside, even very small children wore hats and caps like their parents, although they were allowed the ease of wearing mittens rather than gloves. Boys kept their hair short, but girls under the age of about ten were allowed to have theirs

long and unbound, at least in the informality of their own homes. Children's shoes generally followed the style of the day, being flat, round-toed and close-fitting to the ankle. Pumps were for indoor wear.

By the start of the seventeenth century, it became more common to dress boys and girls alike in frocks until the age of about six, at which time boys were put into breeches and doublets. This was referred to as "breeching." In family portraits which include small children, it is often difficult to tell boys from girls.

The teenage Henry Stuart, Lord Darnley, wears elegant court dress while his brother Charles is still in the skirts of a six-year-old.

Chapter 4: Dressing Up

The severity of Queen Elizabeth's shaved forehead was always offset by pearls or other jewels in the hair.

Hair and Makeup

The most valued attribute for wealthy Elizabethans was pale skin. This demonstrated that one did no outdoor work: suntanned faces were for farmworkers. Brunettes were out of fashion and, while the red-haired Queen Elizabeth popularized that color, the ideal was white skin and golden hair, set off by red lips and sparkling eyes. To achieve this look, people risked injury from cosmetics made of alarmingly dangerous substances. Mercury was used as a face pack to leave the skin soft, while men and women both bleached their skin with lemon juice and rosewater and their hair with urine.

Makeup

Like their dress, women's makeup was highly artificial. Faces were coated with a whitening foundation mixed from white lead and vinegar, and sometimes finished with a glaze of egg white, which dried to a mask. This hid not only wrinkles but the ravages of smallpox and other disfiguring diseases. Face paint, or fucus, included lipstick made of cochineal or vermilion (mercuric sulphide), and kohl to encircle eyes already brightened by drops of belladonna (deadly nightshade). The continued use of white lead dried up the skin and poisoned the system, at best leaving women wrinkled, gray, and haggard, and at worst leading to an early death. Although these dangers were well known, fashion again triumphed over sense.

Elizabethan literature is full of bitingly satirical comments on the artificiality of women's appearance. Hamlet's "God hath given you one face and you make yourselves another" is mild compared to Ben

A Recipe for Blotchy Patches on the Face

"Take a pint of distilled vinegar, lay in it two new-laid eggs in their shell, three spoonfuls of flowers of brimstone. Leave for three days, use this liquid with a cloth, rubbing the place three or four times every day; in three or four days it commonly helps. Put some bran in your cloth before you moisten it in the solution, rolling it into the shape of a small ball."
from *Delights for Ladies* by Sir Hugh Plat (1609).

The drawings in herbals and other "books of receipts" were botanically accurate as well as decorative and beautifully drawn.

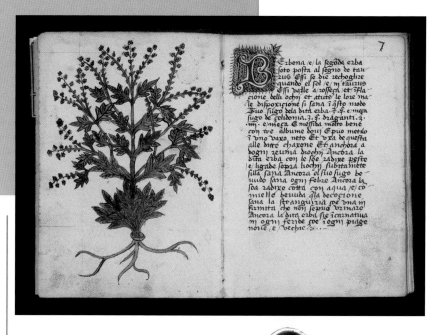

Jonson, who wanted to know: "which lady had her own face to lie with her a-nights, and which not; who put off her teeth with their clothes in court, who their hair, who their complexion, and in which box they put it . . ."

Women's Hairstyles

Women wore their hair braided behind the head and fluffed out in front over the temples. A high, aristocratic forehead was much prized, and to achieve this effect hair was often shaved or plucked at the front. Queen Elizabeth herself favored this style. As the century wore on, hairstyles gradually became more elaborate and higher, with more extravagant curling. Wigs of dyed horsehair were worn, and many women—including the queen—also used false hair to pad out their chosen style. They enhanced the effect with hair bodkins—jeweled brooches on wire pins—stuck into their hair.

Men's Hairstyles

While collars and ruffs were worn high, men's hair was generally cut short and complemented by neatly trimmed beards and moustaches. Very few young men were clean shaven. In the 1560s, beards were rounded, but gradually they became more pointed until, by the 1590s, they had become forked or spade shaped. As falling collars replaced ruffs by the end of the century, hair was worn longer, in loose curls.

This miniature portrait shows the neatly trimmed beard and moustache of the mid-century.

Jewelry

In addition to what we would call decorative jewelry—necklaces, rings, bracelets, brooches, and earrings—Elizabethans carried their wealth sewn to their clothes. Jewels appeared on belts, buttons, hatbands, hairpins, shoes, and garters. Gold, precious stones, and—the latest craze—enameling, were everywhere. There were often several of these combined in one brooch or pendant.

Precious Stones

Of all the precious stones imported from the East, pearls were the declared favorite of Queen Elizabeth, as a symbol of her virginity. Pearls were worn as earrings, set in

brooches, or—most popularly— in long ropes which hung down below the waist, pinned to the skirt in loops. Emeralds, rubies, and diamonds were also popular, but the cutting techniques were still quite rudimentary, and for maximum effect these precious stones tended to be sewn on black velvet rather than worn alone. Glass beads, imported from Venice, were highly prized. In keeping with the taste for the fantastic, tiny pins shaped like butterflies or insects were worn on ruffs or as hairpins.

Earrings were surprisingly discreet: a single teardrop pearl was preferred. Women wore a pair, but men strictly wore only one, usually in the left ear. Multiple strands of pearls or other beads could be wound several times around the wrist as a bracelet.

Brooches and Pendants

Enameled brooches and pendants could be worn on chains round the neck or pinned to the bodice or doublet. Women often wore them low, so that they were framed by the stomacher of the bodice. Sometimes two brooches would be connected by loops of pearls or chains. Men often wore theirs pinned in their hats. Popular shapes included animals, flowers, and ships. The latter were especially fashionable around the time of the threatened invasion of England by the Spanish Armada in 1588. Double brooches were very popular. These included a smaller image of, for example, a galleon

Anyone sitting for a formal portrait would be sure to wear as much fine jewelry as possible in order to indicate their wealth and status.

dangling on a chain beneath linked family initials. Many people wore miniature portraits on ribbons. The portrait might be of a spouse or—for the politically astute—the queen. A gift of jewelry from the monarch was a mark of favor and usually took the form of her initials.

Middle- and Lower-Class Jewelry

As with clothing, the middle classes copied the fashions of their social superiors. However, their jewelry was rendered in inexpensive metals such as pewter, and was composed of imitation pearls or semiprecious stones like garnets, moonstones, and opals.

The hard life of the laborer left little space for personal adornment. Working people might wear a carved wooden cross (although not a crucifix, as this was considered a Catholic symbol) on a ribbon, or a simple necklace of beads made of bone or wood. Few working-class women had the luxury of a wedding ring.

At a time when men kept their hair short, it was very fashionable to wear a single earring.

Costume jewelry like this was made not for the aristocracy but for rich merchants and their wives.

Rings and Things

Curiously, portraits either show rings worn on virtually every finger, including the thumb, or no rings at all, not even a wedding band. Usually only upper-class women wore wedding bands. Widows were expected to remove their wedding rings, as they were no longer considered to have been married. However, they were allowed a mourning ring, which contained a lock of the loved one's hair. Perfume was also often contained in a ring. Some engagement rings had mottoes or declarations of fidelity inscribed on the inside of the band, usually in French or Latin.

Special Occasions

Weddings

Marriage for the upper classes was a civil and a religious occasion, but hardly a sentimental one. Although there were ostentatious displays of finery and lavish entertainment, the white bridal dress was unknown until the nineteenth century. An Elizabethan bride and groom simply wore a particularly fine version of ordinary dress, which would often be worn again for special occasions in future years. The bride wore flowers in her hair and carried a bridal wreath of rosemary and roses. After the ceremony, she wore the wreath on her head as a coronet, a custom retained by all social classes.

Among the upper and middle classes, marriages (and sometimes engagements) were commemorated with individual portraits of the bride and groom in their finery, which have survived as valuable records of fashion. A number of portraits also exist of women who are clearly pregnant, and recent studies suggest that these were commissioned by loving husbands only too aware that their wives might not survive the ordeal ahead. In some cases, they may have been painted as a sad memorial after the wife's death in childbirth. Some of the sitters wear loose-bodied gowns, a rare and welcome concession to nature.

Mourning Clothes

Although white was not yet associated with marriage, black was already the color of mourning. A

The Art of Giving

Special occasions like weddings, as well as the yearly festivals of Christmas and New Year, were marked by the presentation of gifts. These often took the form of expensive accessories, such as fine gloves and stockings. Queen Elizabeth's Wardrobe Accounts record that she received many pairs of these rather intimate garments as New Year gifts from courtiers: in 1588 one pair was "carnation pink, clocked with gold and silver." Gloves were most commonly given at weddings. In Ben Jonson's play *The Silent Woman*, disgruntled guests complain that they see no sign of the promised wedding festivities: "Where be our scarves, and our gloves?"

widow was expected to adopt a black gown and hide her hair under a hood for quite long periods, or until she married again. Embroidery was allowed as long as it was restrained: blackwork patterns were considered particularly suitable here, and discreet jet beads were the only kind of jewelry thought proper.

Ceremonial Dress

The Elizabethan love of theatricality showed itself in the frequency of ceremonial occasions. One of the most impressive was when the twenty-six men appointed by the queen to the Order of the Garter walked in

The procession in which Queen Elizabeth was carried to the palace of Whitehall was an occasion for theatrical splendor.

The grave, middle-aged members of the Court of Wards and Liveries are wearing full formal attire for their meeting.

procession to the chapel at Windsor on St. George's Day. Ceremonial dress was consciously that of a bygone age, in order to give the participants an air of authority. A long velvet gown was worn over the doublet, and over that a floor-length velvet mantle. Those who were members of the exclusive Order wore its deep collar under their ruff. Officers of state, and older men, wore similarly antiquated outfits of black gowns and either tall "flowerpot" hats or velvet caps with a coif beneath. Chains of office and the insignia of various orders confirmed each man's rank.

Men who had been in military service were permitted to wear a combination of armor and civilian dress on special occasions. A gorget, or deep metal collar, was worn below the ruff and perhaps a sash crosswise over the doublet.

Dressing Up

Wherever Queen Elizabeth went she was entertained with lavish pageants recreating significant moments in English history or classical legends. These were often on a vast scale. When she visited Kenilworth in 1575, the entire castle was converted into a miniature fantasy kingdom with a mermaid splashing in the moat, jousting knights, and a mock country wedding. In 1591, the Earl of Hertford created an artificial lake on which he staged a mock sea battle and firework display for her delight.

Masques

The queen and her courtiers also participated in masques at court. The masque was a short interlude combining music, dance, and spectacle, usually illustrating some philosophical or classical allusion. They had titles like "The Golden Age Restored" or "Pleasure Reconciled to Virtue." The general aim was to flatter the queen by suggesting that her ancestry stemmed back to classical times, confirming her position as an absolute monarch to whom even gods and goddesses would pay homage.

These entertainments were above all an opportunity for people who spent their days buttoned up in stiff and constricting court dress to relax and—literally—let their hair down. Women left their hair unbound or wore long, blond wigs. The loose, flowing garments they wore were sometimes startlingly revealing. To preserve modesty, however, their identities were concealed by face masks.

Tournaments

Another excuse for dressing up came with the revival of the tournament, the great medieval pageant of chivalry featuring armed knights jousting on horseback. Henry VIII had encouraged jousting and other events of competitive horsemanship

Tournament armor was just as elaborate as court dress, the best being imported from master armorers in Italy.

as a means of controlling the energy of the young aristocracy, and Elizabeth wisely continued this policy. The grandest events were the Accession Day Tournaments, held each November on the anniversary of Queen Elizabeth's accession to the throne. Most of the armor and weapons, like the long jousting lance, were already many years out of date.

Pastoral Romances

In the tournaments the Elizabethans were consciously creating their own version of their past. Another example of this was the fashion for pastoral romances. The rapid urbanization of England was already causing a nostalgia for the countryside. Beyond the hothouse atmosphere of the court, with its webs of intrigue and favoritism, courtiers imagined country folk leading simple lives of honest toil among their flocks and herds. They tried to recreate this in pastoral entertainments in which they dressed up as shepherds. At the same time,

real country girls like Perdita in Shakespeare's *The Winter's Tale* were dressing up as goddesses of nature to preside over their own festivals such as the end of sheep shearing.

Although these masquers are in contemporary dress, the costumes would be of light fabrics to allow for strenuous dancing.

The Masque of Blackness

"The masquers were placed in a great concave shell, like mother-of-pearl, curiously made to move on those waters, and rise with the billow . . . on sides of the shell did swim six huge sea-monsters, varied in their shapes and dispositions, bearing on their backs the twelve torch-bearers. . . . The attire of the masquers was alike in all, without difference; the colors azure and silver, their hair thick and curled upright in tresses, like pyramids, but returned on top with a scroll and antique dressing of feathers and jewels interlaced with ropes of pearl. . . . For the light-bearers, sea-green, waved about the skirts with gold and silver; their hair loose and flowing, garlanded with sea-grass, and that stuck with branches of coral. These thus presented, the scene behind seemed a vast sea . . ."

Presented at Whitehall on Twelfth Night, 1605

Chapter 5: Casual Clothing

Traveling Clothes, Outdoor Wear, and Keeping Warm

Traveling in Elizabethan times was not for the fainthearted. Highwaymen were a constant hazard, and in the miles of open country between towns, roads were bad and apt to be waterlogged in winter. Inns were few and far from luxurious. The better-off travelers went by horse, and the lucky few in carriages, where they were at least protected from the weather. Poorer folk walked or rode in an open carrier's cart. Protective clothing, boots, and overcoats were essential. Traveling was certainly not to be undertaken in the kind of finery people wore in town or at home.

Unlike today, when fur is worn on the outside for display, the ermine lining of young Edward VI's gown served mostly for warmth.

Clothes for Riding

For riding, men substituted a full-length cloak for the more elegant waist-length version they wore indoors. Long cloaks were slit at the back or sides for convenience on horseback. Other alternatives for horsemen were the leather jerkin and the gabardine, a long, wide coat with wide sleeves. Boots were only worn for riding, never indoors and never by women. The traveling woman would put on a protective over-skirt, or safeguard. If she were lucky, she

The English Wool Trade

Wool from English sheep supplied warm clothing for the home market and cloth to be traded abroad. This was vital to the English economy. From 1558, however, when the English lost control of Calais, the market for wool in France was lost. Bruges and Antwerp in the Netherlands were also thriving centers of the cloth trade, but political tension between England and the Spanish-ruled Netherlands soon closed these markets too. English traders, forced to look farther afield, began opening up trade routes as far as India, trading English wool for silks and spices. In 1600 Queen Elizabeth granted the charter which created the great East India Company.

might have a fur wrap. Another option was the mantle, a loose, sleeveless over-garment made of wool or velvet which draped in folds, similar to a poncho. The mantle went in and out of style during the period, but was the height of fashion between 1580 and 1600.

Dressing for Warmth

Elizabethan houses, and even royal palaces, tended to be chilly places, and people often wore quite substantial clothing indoors. For indoor wear, as well as for traveling, it was still fashionable for women to add a gown over the skirt and bodice. The fitted "close-bodied gown," favorite style of Mary Tudor, lingered on in some parts of the country, but elsewhere had been replaced by the "loose-bodied" variety, often sleeveless, which fell in folds to the floor.

Few young men would be seen in public wearing a gown other than on a formal or ceremonial occasion. Gowns were considered more suitable for the less robust older man or for certain professions. Characters

in Shakespeare's *The Merry Wives of Windsor* are surprised to see the schoolteacher out without his gown: "Youthful still," comments one, "in your doublet and hose this raw rheumatic day?"

Furs of all kinds remained in fashion throughout the period, prized for their luxurious feel as much as for their warmth. They were hardly ever worn alone but were used to line a gown or as an edging for sleeves. Sable and ermine, the most luxurious, were worn only by royalty. Squirrel and beaver were used by the upper classes, and lamb, rabbit, cat, or fox were for the middle classes. Ordinary folk made do with lambskin or sheepskin.

Fashion was far from the minds of most people when faced with a long walk in rough conditions.

Underclothes and Nightwear

As we have seen, Elizabethans cared little about what went into the padding of their clothes as long as the surface effect was acceptable. Similarly, they cared little for underclothing that could not be seen and admired. The modern concept of "fashionable underwear" did not yet exist. The function of underclothes was simply to protect expensive outer garments from sweat, so that they did not have to be cleaned so often. Heavy woolen garments were hard to wash and took a long time to dry, while jeweled brocades and other rich fabrics were virtually impossible to clean.

Undershirts and Drawers

For this reason, underclothing tended to be utilitarian. Both sexes wore a linen undershirt or chemise, and knee-length, white linen drawers, which had openings at the front and the back, tied with ribbons. Drawers were originally worn only by women of easy virtue, but during the sixteenth century, largely as a result of the popularity of horseback riding, it became acceptable for women of all classes to wear them.

Shirts often extended above the neckline and wrists of the doublet to prevent brocades and jewel-encrusted fabrics from chafing the skin. The linen used for shirts was as fine as one could afford. The fashion was for voluminous shirts and close-fitting doublets, and the finer the linen the baggier the shirt could be. Fine linen could also be more easily pulled through the slashings of a doublet. Shirts and chemises were almost invariably white and were kept pristine. Perhaps surprisingly, in an age when personal hygiene was not a top priority, people were scrupulous about washing their linen.

Sleepwear

Underclothes usually doubled as nightclothes, especially among the

The "unknown man" in this famous miniature, in his undershirt and with hair unkempt, is a rare example of an Elizabethan in a state of undress.

lower classes. Generally speaking, *nightgown* did not mean bedwear, but a garment for informal wear around the home, similar to *leisurewear* today.

Stockings

The most visible items of underwear were stockings. The best were hand-knitted from silk, the less expensive from worsted (wool). In 1560 Queen Elizabeth was given her first pair of silk stockings by one of her ladies, Alice Montagu, and declared: "Hence forth I will wear no more cloth stockings." As an indication of how valuable stockings were, even the queen had hers mended: wardrobe accounts for 1597 show "new feet knitted for four pairs white worsted hose clocked with gold, silver and silk." She also had them re-dyed in newly fashionable colors. Plain stocks were often worn under the fashionable ones for warmth. Mary Queen of Scots went to the scaffold wearing "blue worsted, edged and clocked with silver, over plain white jersey hose," held up with green garters.

Male and female underwear was almost identical: in a Ben Jonson play a husband borrows his wife's smock while she washes his shirt.

The Stocking Machine

In 1589, a Nottingham man called William Lee invented a revolutionary new machine for knitting stockings. He proudly showed it to Queen Elizabeth, hoping to be granted a patent. The queen, however, declared herself disappointed at the coarse quality, and refused, although the real reason may have been that she wanted to protect the hand-knitting industry. Lee moved to France where he died a disappointed man, but his partner reintroduced some of the machines to England and set up a business in Nottingham. By the end of the seventeenth century, stocking-knitting machines were operating all over Europe. A model of Lee's machine can be seen in London's Science Museum.

Chapter 6: Work Clothes and Uniforms

Military Clothing

The Buff Jerkin

Since there was no standing army in Elizabethan England, military uniforms did not yet exist. The universal garment of the foot soldier was the buff jerkin. This was similar to a doublet but much longer; it had no collar and was either laced or buttoned to the waist. The name buff actually signified buffalo leather, but in practice the jerkins were generally made of oiled ox hide. For serious protection in warfare, however, a soldier might wear a jack, which was a jerkin that contained metal plates, quilted over with leather or canvas.

The plain buff jerkin was originally used exclusively by soldiers, because it was tough and could withstand sword cuts. However, it soon became a fashion item, worn by young men about town. It was also the uniform of the Watch, the local constabulary who patrolled towns at night.

Armor

By Elizabeth's time, the full metal armor worn by knights was in decline and appeared mainly at tournaments. Improvements in firearms meant that to remain bulletproof, armor had become so heavy that it was virtually unwearable. Nevertheless, each town was required by law to keep a supply of armor in store, in case troops had to be recruited in an emergency. However, for the most part this consisted of outdated breastplates and helmets.

The costume of the average soldier changed very little throughout the sixteenth century.

The Mandilion

One of the strangest fashions of the 1580s was for a garment called the mandilion, a loose, hip-length military jacket which buttoned up the front and had slits up the sides. It could be thrown casually over the shoulders with the sleeves hanging, but when adapted to civilian wear it typifies the vogue for useless artifice. It was usually worn sideways, buttoned up so that the front and back panels covered the shoulders and the sleeves hung down over the chest and back. Nevertheless, it cut quite a dash. One of Queen Elizabeth's progresses included "threescore of the most comelie yong men of the cities, as bachelers apparelled all in black sattyn doublets, blacke hose, blacke taffeta hattes and yeallowe bandes, and their universall liverie was a mandylion of purple taffeta, layde aboute with silver lace . . .".

There are many portraits of Elizabethan men who had themselves painted in tournament armor. These reveal that armor had begun to follow the style of civilian fashion: breastplates shaped like peascod doublets were worn with ruffs, collars, and frilly wristbands. Other items of military wear were eagerly adopted as peacetime fashion items. The baldric, a belt worn from one shoulder to the opposite hip and intended to carry a powder horn (for gunpowder) or other implements, now carried a purse. Colored scarves and sashes, originally a means of identification in battle, were worn across the chest or around the waist.

Sailors

Like the soldier, the Elizabethan sailor had no distinguishing uniform. The most common outfit seems to have been a short, loose coat and baggy, knee-length breeches worn with an unstarched ruff and a high, brimless fur hat. Portraits of senior naval men and explorers, like Drake, Hawkins, and Frobisher, show them wearing a more practical version of court dress, with breeches instead of hose below the doublet. Sailors always wore a gold earring, the tradition being that this piece of gold would pay their passage into the underworld if they were drowned.

Sir Martin Frobisher, the famous seafarer and explorer, wears a sleeveless buff jerkin over his doublet.

Ecclesiastical Clothing

With the dissolution of the monasteries, Henry VIII swept away many of the visual reminders of England's Roman Catholic past, including church statues and the more ostentatious vestments of the clergy. Until this time the English priest had been as richly dressed as his counterparts in France or Italy, and English ecclesiastical needlework, or Opus Anglicanum as it was known, was famed throughout Europe. This embroidery, usually employing gold and silver thread and seed pearls on velvet, brocade, or cloth of gold, was worked into elaborate designs on the cope, a semicircular cape worn over other vestments. Popular images were flowers, birds, and the twining tendrils of the "tree of Jesse" from the Bible.

Ceremonial Occasions

Although England was now officially Protestant, Queen Elizabeth chose to interpret the laws fairly loosely. As long as people were loyal to the state she turned a blind eye to those continuing to practice Catholicism in private. She allowed the Church of England clergy to retain many of the old vestments, including their fine copes and colorful robes. On ceremonial occasions, the clergy made a grand appearance. An observer of Queen Elizabeth at a court ceremony in 1602 noted: "The Bishop of London in his cope delivered her a book . . . in the presence of all the prebends and churchmen, who attended her Highness in very rich copes." And again, on the occasion of the queen's second Parliament, there were: "Bishops . . . riding in their robes of scarlet lined, and hoods down their backs of miniver."

The Puritans

These concessions to "Popish" tradition greatly upset the Puritans, extreme Protestants who wished to purify the Church of all aspects of Catholicism. They wanted to abolish

Figures represented in effigy on tombs usually wore intentionally old-fashioned dress to give them an air of solemn gravity.

Ecclesiastical Embroidery

When church property was dispersed, stones and building materials were eagerly seized by the new landowners and incorporated into their new houses. In the same way, many of the richly embroidered ecclesiastical vestments appeared on the market and were acquired by women to be reused as panels in dresses or household hangings. Bess of Hardwick and Mary Queen of Scots acquired some of these embroideries, and also used them as patterns for their own work. Many other church vestments were destroyed when their valuable gold and silver thread was torn out and melted down.

not only the vestments but also the whole hierarchy of the Church. The Puritans adopted very sober dress, wearing only black suits and white shirts, with tall hats and soft, falling collars. They frowned on most pleasurable pursuits like music, sports, and dancing. As usual, this earned them the mockery of playwrights.

Ordinary Dress

For ordinary occasions, churchmen—like lawyers and doctors—generally wore black. When outdoors they wore a cassock, a plain, full-length gown lined with fur, and a four-cornered biretta-style hat. Parish parsons were generally poor. Many were ex-monks no longer allowed to wear habits. To officiate at services they wore the surplice, a white, wide-sleeved gown, over the cassock.

Despite Elizabeth's relaxed attitude, she was determined that religion should remain an integral part of English life. Attendance at church was compulsory, on pain of a shilling fine—almost half a laborer's weekly wage. Catholicism remained strong as an underground movement, and priests continued to celebrate mass secretly in family chapels. However, the penalties for this grew more harsh as Elizabeth became convinced that Catholics were plotting against her.

Wiliam Warham, Archbishop of Canterbury, wears a relatively simple fur-trimmed cassock, but the miter seen behind him is elaborately embroidered.

Servants

In Elizabethan society, everybody knew their place. There were class divisions among servants just as there were among their superiors, and these were made clear by their clothing. Servants in aristocratic families dressed well, especially in public, as they were representatives of their masters. Personal servants were particularly fortunate because their employers handed down their cast-off clothing. To avoid the embarrassment of servants being mistaken for their betters, the clothes were usually a few years behind current fashion.

Livery

Male servants in a large household wore livery, a uniform with the family badge embroidered on the sleeve or on the doublet. Looking back from 1617, the traveler and writer Fynes Moryson noted that:

"The servants of Gentlemen were wont to weare blew coats, with their Masters badge of silver on the left sleeve: but now they most commonly weare clokes garded with lace, all the servants of one family wearing the same livery for color and ornament; and for the rest, are apparrelled with no lesse pride and inconstancie of fashion then other degrees."

Colors

Blue was the color particularly associated with servants, although sober shades of brown or gray were also acceptable. The poorer class of domestic servants wore neat but plain woolen clothing with caps and aprons.

Supply of Uniforms

Employers were responsible for supplying their servants' clothing as part of their wages. The female servant of a country gentleman in Yorkshire in the 1590s was paid thirteen shillings a year, plus four shillings in livery. Another household account from the same period itemizes: "A pair of knit hose—10p; a pair of shoes—13p; for making a jerkin, doublet, and breeches for the kitchen boy—16p." Alice Gee, in Manchester, received forty shillings and a gown on the death of her master, confirming that clothing was an integral part of the economy.

Upper-Class Servants

As most people realized that personal advancement was achieved through the patronage of the powerful, there

The three Browne brothers are dressed in the height of fashion for 1598 while their page wears an outdated suit probably handed down by his master.

Sumptuary Laws

The main reason given for the introduction of sumptuary laws was to control imports and protect local trades. However, these laws were also attempts by the government to maintain the social hierarchy. The population was divided into nine categories, each with a detailed description of the clothing and fabrics they were allowed to wear. Offenders were fined. There were ten proclamations between 1559 and 1597. These decreed that, for example: only the nobility could wear imported wool; only those with more than £200 in income could wear velvet, embroidery, or decoration with gold, silver, or silk; apprentices could not wear gloves costing more than one shilling, or gloves with fingers or with fancy trimmings. The 1571 Cappers Act decreed that every male over the age of six was to wear a cap of English wool on Sundays and Holy Days. Not surprisingly, these laws were virtually impossible to enforce and were treated with disdain by most of the population.

A black servant in the household was a status symbol: many went on to become wealthy men in their own right.

However, a certain amount of uniformity was encouraged, and the maids of honor who surrounded the queen on formal occasions usually dressed in identical outfits to make a harmonious scene.

was no shame in starting out as a servant. The aristocracy, in fact, often employed members of their own families as servants in their enormous households. Similarly, even minor attendants at court were invariably minor aristocrats and perfectly able to purchase their own fine clothes.

This keeper of hounds would be used to the company of the aristocracy on hunting expeditions and his clothing is suitably refined.

Trades and Professions

The Apprentices Act

Apprentices were bound by their own sumptuary laws. The Apprentices Act of 1582 prevented them from wearing any clothes other than those supplied by their masters. Prohibited clothing included: any kind of fancy ruff; a doublet made of anything other than canvas, fustian, sackcloth, English leather, or wool, and with any kind of decoration in gold, silver, or silk; stockings in any color but white, blue, or russet; breeches which did not match their doublet; any coat other than a plain one of cloth or leather, with no edging or silk about it; pumps, slippers, or shoes of anything but English leather, and with no decoration; garters of anything but plain leather. They could not carry a sword, a dagger, or any other weapon, nor wear a ring, jewelry, gold, silver, or silk "in any part of his apparel." Not surprisingly, the apprentices were frequently in revolt.

Professionals

Doctors, lawyers, and other professional men were easily distinguishable as they continued to wear the gown, a garment fashionable for 150 years but now generally considered passé. Fur-or velvet-lined and trimmed, the gown fell to the ankle in folds from a fitted yoke and had hanging sleeves with a slit for the arms—it is the ancestor of today's academic gown. Worn with the gown was a coif or under cap of linen, which fitted close to the head and fastened under the chin. Elderly men were permitted the association with professionals as a mark of respect, and wore similar clothing.

The doctor's fur-lined gown was as much a symbol of his profession as the falconer's leather jerkin and gauntlets.

Minor professionals, such as schoolteachers, were frequently poor and their clothes were correspondingly neat but shabby. Huntsmen and falconers, who had contact with the aristocracy, were considered professionals and dressed like their betters but in plainer style.

Tradespeople

Tradesmen could often be identified by the kind of apron they wore. Carpenters and blacksmiths, working with sharp tools, wore thick leather for protection, while butchers and cooks wore coarse linen aprons which were easily washable. Farmers and fisherfolk wore long leather leggings called cockers for wading in mud. In those days it was common to see fishwives selling their recent catches on the banks of the Thames.

Not surprisingly, the tradesmen and women with the most interest in being well dressed were those connected with the cloth trade. A stapler bought and sold raw wool; a draper was a wholesale dealer in cloth, and sold ready-made garments; and a mercer was the retailer who kept the local fabric shop.

Almost everybody wore a headcovering of some sort when out of doors, but caps especially identified tradesmen and apprentices. The 1571 Cappers Act, which was intended to boost the woolen cap-makers' business, ensured that caps were firmly associated with trade.

Apprentices

Apprentices were rarely poor boys but usually the younger sons of well-off families hoping for farther advancement. As the historian John Stow remarked, they were "often children of gentlemen and persons of good quality . . . [who in their free time] affected to go in costly apparel and wear weapons and frequent schools of dancing, fencing and music." In the booming world of Elizabethan commerce there were fortunes to be made by enterprising young men willing to work their way up through a business. The comedy *Eastward Ho!* is just one of many plays showing the rags-to-riches progress of a bright lad-about-town.

The restrained elegance of this tailor would have been a good advertisement for his trade. He carries his cutting shears in his right hand.

Chapter 7: The Jacobeans

A New Monarch

Queen Elizabeth died in 1603 at the age of seventy. Having no heir, she was succeeded by James VI of Scotland, who became James I of England. The period of his reign became known as the Jacobean era. For the first years of the new reign, clothing remained much the same: formal and full of artifice. James, although physically rather unattractive, loved luxury and spent lavishly on clothing and ceremonial events: the coronation alone cost over £20,000.

The king also surrounded himself with a crowd of young male courtiers who were eager to keep up with the latest fashions. James's queen, Anne of Denmark, far outdid Queen Elizabeth in her fondness for clothes, jewelry, and entertainment. Enormous amounts of money were spent on court masques alone, which reached new heights of lavishness. The reign of King James was characterized by riotous living and lavish expenditure, which threatened to bankrupt the country.

Changing Styles

As the new century progressed, dress gradually became more relaxed. Dark colors were still popular but there was less embroidery and the general cut of clothing was becoming less extreme. The peascod doublet and its stuffing disappeared, giving way to a softer doublet with a high waist and long skirts. Trunk hose fell from favor, to be replaced almost universally by longer, loosely pleated breeches. These were at first knee-length, but by about 1620 they had become longer and slimmer fitting, looking more like modern trousers. As ruffs were gradually abandoned, the standing band collar became larger and softer until, by 1620, it lay over the shoulders, broad and lacy. Men's hair was allowed to grow longer and, ideally, fall into waves.

Women's bodies were finally released from the torture of whalebone, padding, and farthingales and began to return to something like a natural shape. Skirts were looser, sleeves

In thirty years, a fashion revolution had occurred. The Countess of Bedford here is wearing the more relaxed fashion of 1638.

wider, and necklines lower. Hair was worn flat on the head, with ringlets or curls at the side.

Extravagance, however, was still very much in evidence in the accessories. In the early years of James's reign men's shoes were colorful and highly ornate. They were fastened by buckles and huge ribbon bows, and their fronts were obscured by large rosettes. Equally bright embroidered stockings were held up by elaborate garters tied under the knee. Hats became taller and more elaborate, and their decoration eventually had to be limited by royal statute. By 1620, however, these extreme fashions had worn themselves out.

In 1625, James died and was succeeded by his son, Charles I. Shortly after his accession Charles married the French-born princess Henrietta Maria, and when she arrived in England with a wardrobe of Parisian elegance, the fashion scene changed completely.

King James's Favorite Hat

Felt hats were the height of fashion throughout the Jacobean period, a trend encouraged by the king himself. The best fur for making felt was beaver, but by the beginning of the 1600s these animals were close to extinction in western Europe, Scandinavia, and Russia, and the fur trade moved to North America. By the early 1700s America had its own thriving hat trade which threatened the home trade in England. The Hat Act of 1732 forbade the export of beaver felt hats made in the colonies and forced Americans to buy British-made goods on which they had to pay heavy taxes. This was one of the grievances that ultimately led to the American Revolution of 1776.

Topping and tailing the members of King James's court, shoes and hats achieved new heights of ridiculousness in his reign, encouraged by the king himself.

Timeline

1554 Philip of Spain visits England to marry Queen Mary. Spanish style becomes fashionable.

1558 The accession of Queen Elizabeth.

1562 The Statutes of Apparel, limiting the wearing of certain clothes and fabrics, are enforced by royal decree.

1564 Starch is introduced to England.

1565 Tobacco is first introduced to England.

1567 London's Royal Exchange, a shopping and trading center, is founded by Thomas Gresham.

1574 The Statutes of Apparel are reinforced, largely to protect British local industries.

1577–8 William Harrison publishes *A Description of England*, commenting on fashion and clothing.

1582 The Apprentices Act severely limits what young apprentices can wear.

1583 Philip Stubbes publishes *An Anatomy of Abuses*, attacking extravagance in fashion and expenditure.

1585 Sir Walter Raleigh's first colony is established in Roanoke, Virginia. News of the exotic costumes of the indigenous population filters back to England.

1587 Mary Queen of Scots, fashion icon and skilled needlewoman, is executed after being implicated in a plot to kill Queen Elizabeth.

1589 William Lee invents a machine for knitting stockings.

1600 The East India Company is established, opening up trade with India and the east.

1601 Poor Law Statutes compel each parish to provide work for the unemployed. Poor women find work in needlework, bleaching, and dyeing.

1603 The death of Queen Elizabeth and the accession of James I.

1615 The publication of *The English Housewife*, a general household manual, including advice on making and caring for clothing.

Glossary

allegorical   Figurative.

allusion   Reference.

apothecary   Chemist.

apparel   Clothing.

appliqué   One material sewn onto another.

archetypal   Typical.

artifice   Cleverness or skill.

belladonna   A drug obtained from the plant, deadly nightshade.

biretta   A stiff, square clerical hat.

blackwork   Embroidery in black thread.

bobbin   A spool or reel.

bodice   The upper part of a woman's dress.

braiding   Ornamental trim.

breeches   Trousers reaching knee-length or just below.

buttonhole stitch   An edging stitch.

carcenet   A necklace resembling a collar.

chain stitch   An embroidery stitch resembling the links of a chain.

chemise   A loose, shirtlike undergarment.

chivalry   A code of behavior followed by medieval knights.

church brasses   Memorial plaques or tablets.

clocked   Embroidered with an ornamental design.

cloth of gold   A fabric woven with real gold thread.

cochineal   A crimson dye obtained from Mexican beetles.

codpiece   A decorated pouch concealing the opening of men's breeches.

coif   A close-fitting cap.

copotain   A high-crowned hat.

dandified   Dressed in the height of fashion.

dandy   A very fashionably dressed man.

décolleté   With a low neckline.

divinity   Theology.

doublet   A man's jacket-like upper garment.

drawer   One who draws copies of patterns.

drawers   Long knickers.

ethereal   As light as air.

falconer   Someone who trains and flies birds of prey.

flax   A plant, the stems of which are used to make linen.

flocks   Lumps of cotton waste.

flounce   Frill.

gable headdress   An English hood with the front shaped like the gable of a house.

galleon   A large sailing ship with masts.

garter   A band around the leg, holding up the stocking.

gathered   Drawn into tiny pleats.

gauntlet   A cuffed glove.

gauze   Transparent, fine fabric.

Gothic   Relating to the Middle Ages, especially the architecture.

haberdasher   A seller of small articles for sewing.

hemp   A plant with tough fibers used to make rough fabric.

hose   Tight-fitting leggings.

itinerant   Traveling from place to place.

jerkin   A sleeveless fitted jacket.

jousting   Combat between two mounted knights.

kohl   A black cosmetic used to darken the eye area.

mantle   A woman's overdress or coat.

melancholy   Sad or thoughtful.

milliner   A hatmaker.

miniver   White fur.

modish   Fashionable.

pantofle   A heeled, backless shoe.

passé   Outdated.

patten   A wooden sandal.

peascod doublet   A men's garment padded into the shape of a peascod at the front.

pleated   Folded.

posterity   Future generations.

prebend   A canon or member of a cathedral.

progress   A royal journey, usually from one great house to another.

rapier   A narrow sword.

Renaissance   The revival of art and learning

beginning in fourteenth-century Europe.

rheumatic Suffering from pain in the joints.

russet A coarse, woolen homespun cloth worn by country people.

satirical Mocking topical issues.

scallop Shell shaped.

seed pearl A tiny pearl.

sequin A tiny piece of shiny metal.

stomacher A decorative v-shaped panel in the bodice.

sumptuary laws Laws intended to control extravagance.

swaddling clothes Strips of linen cloth in which a baby was wrapped.

taffeta A thin, crisp silk fabric.

tassel A group of threads tied together in a knot.

tilt yard An enclosure where jousting or other feats of horsemanship took place.

tournament A sporting contest, mainly between mounted opponents.

vermilion Bright orange-red.

vestment An ecclesiastical robe.

worsted A wool fabric with a smooth surface and no nap.

Further Information

Reference Sources

Arnold, Janet, *Patterns of Fashion: the Cut and Construction of Clothes for Men and Women c.1560–1620* (Drama Publishing, 1985)

Arnold, Janet, *Queen Elizabeth's Wardrobe Unlocked* (Quite Specific Media Group, 2001)

Brooks Picken, Mary, *A Dictionary of Costume and Fashion: Historic and Modern* (Dover, 1999)

Cosgrave, Bronwyn, *The Complete History of Costume & Fashion: From Ancient Egypt to the Present Day* (Checkmark Books, 2001)

Laver, James, *Costume and Fashion* (Thames and Hudson World of Art, 2002)

Norris, Herbert, *Tudor Costume and Fashion* (Dover, 1997)

Nunn, Joan, *Fashion in Costume 1200–2000* (New Amsterdam Books, 2000)

Racinet, Albert and Auguste, *Historic Encyclopedia of Costumes* (Checkmark Books, 1995)

Racinet, Auguste, *Costume History* (Taschen, 2003)

Tortora, Phyllis G. and Eubank, Keith, *A Survey of Historic Costume* (Fairchild, 1998)

Vecellio, Cesare, *Vecellio's Renaissance Costume Book* (Dover, 1977)

Weiditz, Christoph, *Authentic Everyday Dress of the Renaissance* (Dover, 1994)

Winter, Janet, *Elizabethan Costuming for the Years 1550–1580* (Other Times, 1991)

Ashelford, Jane (illustrator), *A Visual History of Costume: The 16th Century* (Batsford, 1983)

Cunnington, Phillis and Buck, Anne, *Children's Costume in England, 1300–1900* (A & C Black, 1965)

Sichel, Marion, *Costume Reference 2: Tudors and Elizabethans* (Batsford, 1977)

Internet Resources

http://www.costumes.org
The Costumer's Manifesto: a general website on the history of costume with links to sites on different cultures, and their costumes. The sixteenth-century costume links page within the site is at
http://www.costumes.org/history/100pages/16thlinks.htm

http://costume.dm.net/
The Elizabethan Costuming Page: the largest of many Elizabethan costume sites, has patterns, photos, how-to, primary sources, and links to many of the other important sites on the subject. It includes a searchable database of Elizabeth's predecessor Mary I's wardrobe accounts, and detailed information on clothing of all classes, both in England and on the continent.

http://www.vertetsable.com/
The Renaissance Tailor is an online library of rare sixteenth- and seventeenth-century tailor's pattern books, with technical commentary and sewing information for using these primary source materials to recreate European dress in these eras.

http://www.thrednedlestrete.com
Resource for historical costumiers.

http://www.elizabethangeek.com/costumereview
Historical portraits and notes.

http://www.fordham.edu/halsall
Tudor history sourcebook, including Harrison's *Description of England.*

http://renaissance.dm.net
Renaissance, The Elizabethan World: everyday life in Tudor England, including fashion.

http://www.blackworkarchives.com/
The Blackwork Embroidery Archives has free printable patterns of this popular Elizabethan form of needlework and its history.

http://www.tudor-portraits.com/
Tudor and Elizabethan portraits.

http://www.shakespeare.org.uk
Shakespeare Birthplace Trust: background information from the plays of Shakespeare and his contemporaries.

http://www.elizabethi.org/us/
Elizabeth R, a site on the sixteenth-century queen, includes many pithy outlines of different aspects of her life, death, and reign, including her clothing.

http://www.renaissance.dm.net/compendium
Life in Tudor England.

http://www.shakespeare.org.uk
Shakespeare Birthplace Trust: background information from the plays of Shakespeare and his contemporaries.

Index